THE LITTLE BOOK OF WOWW!™

WOWING BY DESIGN!

Be WOWW!

Michelle Hoskin
The WOWW! Coach™

Mike Morrow
Certified Financial Planner®

First published in 2016

Published by:
Michelle Hoskin
michelle@standardsinternational.co.uk
+44 (0)1462 790894
5 The Granary, Fairclough Hall Farm,
Weston, Hertfordshire SG4 7DP, UK

and

Mike Morrow
mike@ideasforadvisors.com
1 807 684 1805
200-905 Tungsten St.
Thunder Bay, ON, Canada P7B 5Z3

Design: Carla Green, Studio C Graphics

ISBN 978-1-5236368-7-7

Anyone who knows me well will know that I am totally obsessed with the concept of WOW!

After spending the last 15 years working with some of the most amazing financial services businesses globally, I continue to be amazed at the lengths these firms will go to WOW!

So what does WOW! look like in today's busy and progressive businesses?

Well, I thought it was about time I pulled together the ideas, tips and tricks which – when implemented – create a five-star client journey.

Plus... luckily for you, I know a man who also has a few WOW! ideas himself. I asked my friend Mike Morrow to share some of his own suggestions, ideas which I know he has tested and used himself with huge success!

It's time to bring the Michelin (or 'Michelle'in') Star concept to our magical profession!

Enjoy, share and go WOW!

Michelle Hoskin
www.standardsinternational.co.uk

First off, big, huge thanks to Michelle! We were delighted when she asked us to co-author *The Little Book of WOWW!™* Over the past ten years, Michelle and I have had the opportunity to speak together at industry and Million Dollar Round Table (MDRT) events as we share the same philosophies that little things have the biggest impact and the unexpected leaves a lasting impression.

Based in Canada and having been a practising financial advisor for over 25 years, I learned early in my career that it is easier to keep existing clients than to find new ones. So I developed many simple yet extremely effective ways to build client loyalty and stand out in our profession's competitive market. We have grown our business successfully by consistently *'wowing'* our clients and prospects because 'WOW' is about doing small things well, consistently and seamlessly, thus making a big and memorable impression on those you care for the most!

The Little Book of WOWW!™ is packed full of practical, easy-to-implement and field-tested ideas and strategies that we promise will make a dramatic difference to you, your business and most importantly your clients. Real ideas, used by real advisors! Share the secrets and keep it close!

Good luck growing your business.

Mike Morrow
www.ideasforadvisors.com

"A tremendous tome of tried and tested tips. Imagine the difference to our businesses and our clients if we could implement just one of these ideas every week? And what if we could implement all 90 in two years? WOWW!"

— Ian Green, Financial Planner, London, UK

"Anyone who has heard Michelle speak knows that from a small package comes a whole load of energy, value and power. This little book is a reflection of its author – it is packed with immediately actionable tips to take your clients' experience of your practice to the next level. Read, act, and watch your clients love you more for it."

— Pete Matthew, Managing Director,
Jacksons Wealth Management

"Times are changing, and faster than ever. In the days of internet and conveyor belt service seemingly taking over, the one area that medium cannot compete in is proper personal service with real people.

We need to ensure we add value at every step along the way – to receive good service is frankly the expected minimum benchmark. To stand out in the crowd, our client must be wowed, and staff must feel proud.

This book is an adviser's bible, and should be on the shelves of every adviser, and become the standard to which we strive. Follow these simple but highly effective tips and watch your business soar, powered by WOWW!"

— David Braithwaite, Managing Director,
Citrus Financial Management

"As a mentor to more than 150 agents worldwide, I'm always looking for a way to give my people an edge out in the field. This book is more than a good read. It's a great tool, but only if you're serious about your success."

— Sol Hicks, Top of the Table Member and Speaker

Contents

The Arrival

1 Think about collecting your clients and guests from the station or even the airport and taking them to your office, or arrange for a car to meet them on arrival. Don't leave them to book their own transport.

2 Make sure your signage and directions to your office or meeting place are clearly marked. You don't want your guests feeling frustrated because they can't find where you are.

3 Put up a personali car or welcome sign outside the office to welcome your clients and guests.

4 If it's raining, meet your guests at their car or taxi with an umbrella that's branded with your company logo. Put the umbrella in an umbrella bag and give it to them to take home as a gift from you.

5 On a good day, we have approximately seven seconds to make an impression! Think about the welcome at your office. Who welcomes your guests? Is it someone smiley and cheerful who represents your company really well? Look at the reception area: is it cluttered? Think about every aspect of your environment and how it might appear to someone arriving for the first time. Think of the welcome that you get in your favourite hotel and restaurant or places where you are made to feel totally welcome and special! Try to repeat it.

6 Have an aroma diffuser in the office so that a calming and relaxing scent greets your clients and guests as they arrive. Have scented candles that match the background fragrance and give them as gifts to those you have a long-term relationship with.

7 Occasionally your guests may arrive late for meetings, maybe in a bit of a fluster; perhaps they've been caught in traffic. Make it part of your process to give them a few moments alone to settle themselves. Your head of hospitality should say, "We'll just give you a few moments to gather your thoughts and get ready for the meeting." The meeting can then start in a calmer manner.

8 Think about having a selection of magazines in your reception area that cater to your guests' personal interests, be it golf, sailing or farming. When clients and guests are welcomed, just say, "We have taken the opportunity to provide a selection of magazines which you may enjoy while you wait."

9 For larger businesses, think about having a video from the business owner playing in reception or available on a tablet or device when clients and guests visit your office. Often, as a business gets bigger, not everyone is able to meet the person who started the business.

10 In case a client or guest has been caught in inclement weather, have a selection of towels ready in the bathroom, and possibly a hairdryer. Lay out some disposable toothbrushes, disposable hairbrushes and small toiletries so that they can freshen up prior to their meeting with you.

11 In your car park, ensure that all allocated parking spaces are clearly identifiable, for example "Client parking – Morrow Financial".

12 During your meeting have one of your team put an envelope under the windscreen wipers of your guest's car with a thank you note, your business card and a gift card for a local coffee shop.

The Office

13 Consider office clutter: take a walk around your office. Do you have a clear desk policy and is it being followed? If not, think about implementing one to keep workspaces and the work environment tidy, not just for clients and guests but also for your team.

14 Don't use your main office or any public meeting rooms as a storage space for old pictures, old computers, boxes of filing or paperwork that is waiting to be archived or destroyed.

15 Keep kitchen and bathroom doors closed at all times. Don't cook or reheat food in an open office. Be mindful of strong-smelling food. Your office should appeal to all five senses when your clients and guests arrive.

16 Make sure there's nothing broken in the office, such as chairs or door handles. Anything that looks amiss in an office will be picked up instantly by your guests. Think about it: if a client sees that a toilet roll holder is hanging off and you haven't cared to fix it, are they going to have confidence and trust in your ability to get them through their financial planning journey?

17 Look closely around your office for chipped wall paint, dirty walls/woodwork or a messy floor. Tidy it; fix it!

18 Have seasonal fruit and fresh flowers in the office. There's nothing more refreshing and enlivening than walking into a bright, sweet-smelling and well-stocked office.

19 Have matching crockery, nice spoons, sugar bowls, milk jugs, teapots and coffee pots. Don't expect your clients and guests – or your team – to make do with any old mug that you picked up at some conference or other. Don't forget glassware – plastic is a no-go!

20 Keep the bathroom tidy; don't use it as a store cupboard for mops and buckets (or private and personal items that nobody really wants to see!).

21 Provide proper towels in the bathroom – no paper towels. Ensure there is a bathroom bin with a sealed lid; have good soap and nice toilet paper. (I know this sounds crazy, but most just have cheap everyday toilet paper. Invest in decent toilet paper!)

22 Don't just focus on the inside of the office – walk from the car park to the front and/or back door. Are there weeds sprouting, broken paving stones, litter? Don't let your guests trip over a step which you know is a hazard. You should also consider the walk from the station(s) and/or offsite parking to your office.

23 Think about your internal dress code. It's not necessarily vital that you wear smart suits on days when you are not expecting guests, but consider a dress code nevertheless. If you have clients who work in a very creative space – media relations, art and design, for example, maybe even theatre or television – formal suits may be inappropriate or look out of place. It's OK to have a dress code and ask your team to comply. It's your company image and brand that are on the line.

24 Work on the basis that nothing is too much trouble! Anything you can do to help serve and take care of your clients and guests will make the environment more hospitable and it will be appreciated.

25 Have a small library in the waiting area. A collection of books should focus on finance, wellbeing and other related topics. After the meeting you can select a book as a gift which may be on a topic that you discussed during the meeting.

26 Laminate a life insurance term rate sheet or other key information and add it to the magazine selection on the waiting room table.

27 Frame any press coverage including interviews (newspapers or magazines) and hang them in or close to the waiting area so all your guests can see and appreciate your expertise!

The Meeting

28 When clients are being invited to a meeting, ask if they'd like to bring anybody else to accompany them, such as their spouse, partner, key family members or just a family friend.

29 When you book a meeting, confirm to your guest how much time will be allocated for it. If you do this in advance, it will help the client with paying for parking, for instance. It will also mean that they can plan their day much better. Don't just confirm the date and the time of a meeting, but also confirm how much time they may need to set aside for it.

30 Consider arranging family meetings. You'll often find that a client's biggest concern is the next generation: can their children manage money? Can they manage debt when they go to university? Suggest a family meeting to discuss the area of finance generally with all key persons present. My parents never taught me about financial planning, but luckily I'm good at managing money. I'm a firm believer that people should talk to family members, particularly their children, about money. Consider how you might add value by doing this proactively.

31 If clients are coming to a busy city or they've travelled some distance to meet you, consider booking them (and their partner if they're travelling together) in for breakfast or lunch at a nice restaurant so the day can become more of an experience for them.

32 Have a menu of drinks and snacks available as well as a fully stocked fridge in your meeting room.

If clients and guests are coming in the morning, provide some pastries, snack bars or fruit. It's a good idea to ask if they have any dietary requirements in advance. If the client or guest is with you over lunchtime, consider providing a sandwich platter or making formal catering arrangements.

33 If clients or guests have children, offer them the option of bringing their children with them and allocate someone to look after them while they meet their adviser and take care of their financial planning. Have a selection of crayons, pencils and sticker books ready – anything that will keep the children busy. This helps to make sure that parents can visit your office at a time that's convenient for them and therefore will speed up the financial planning process!

34 If a client has visited you before, remember their drink preferences and ask, "Would you like an Earl Grey/smoothie/black coffee/tea with one sugar again?" Just show that you care enough to remember the small details.

35 If you're in a meeting for longer than 45 minutes, it should be policy that someone from your team (ideally, the person in charge of hospitality) knocks gently on the door to ask if anyone would like more refreshments. This creates an opportunity to have a refreshment and/or bathroom break, as well as a chance to adjust the meeting agenda or bring discussions to a close.

36 Consider audio recording your meetings so that anyone who is unable to be there can listen to the meeting. Often compliance is against this; however, I would ask: if it can't be recorded, should it be said?

37 When you prepare documentation in advance, such as meeting summaries and financial plans, think about your clients individually. Do you have an older client with sight problems? Perhaps a large font size for documents or an audio recording of a meeting would be helpful. This is a great way of really involving clients in the process. Also ask if they would like you to send a copy of the documentation to any significant third parties.

38 Consider giving clients a personalised safekeeping file for their documents to take away with them. This should have your company logo on it, along with your full contact information so they can retrieve your details easily.

39 If clients and guests have parked in your car park or a car park close by, ask them towards the end of the meeting if they would like to have their car brought round. If they have paid to park close by, maybe ask if they would like you to arrange to put more money on their parking ticket/meter, so as not to disturb the meeting.

40 When you conclude a meeting, ensure that the next meeting is confirmed and booked in the diary. Send them an electronic invite or give them a pre-filled and branded appointment card to take away with them. Remember it is easier to book a meeting and reschedule rather than have to try to get it in the diary in the first place.

41 Whatever you do, finish well: offer a strong handshake, confident confirmation and details of what's going to happen next. Don't leave a client hanging, wondering what's going to happen after the meeting or next in their journey.

42 Consider personally introducing clients and guests to key members of your team. This will enhance the client journey by making sure they meet the people who will deal with their financial planning requirements as their relationship with you develops.

43 Walk all of your clients and guests out of your building, even to their car/ taxi – don't just see them to the nearest door or into the lift. Show them that you really care.

44 You or your team should call your client or guest a day before their meeting to confirm that everything is still OK. Why not take it one step further by emailing them the meeting agenda in advance? This will help them prepare for the topics that you will be discussing so that there are no surprises and they can duly consider things beforehand.

45 Message your clients or guests with a note a couple of hours before the meeting telling them you are looking forward to seeing or speaking with them.

46 During the meeting reference articles or white papers that support your advice and recommendations. Have these available for your client to take home with them to use as reference points later on.

47 Ensure that any presentations you give are engaging, interesting and effective. Use pictures and diagrams to explain complicated financial concepts but remember, less is definitely more.

48 Hand-deliver big documents and policies. Go big on personal service and it will leave a lasting impression.

49 Documents should be presented in a customised quality wallet or handcrafted case. Include a congratulatory letter and any supporting information.

50 If you haven't already done so, as you are leaving the meeting room at the end of the meeting make a point to stop by the book library and give your client or guest a book that relates to the meeting topic(s).

Going the Extra Mile

51 During my own financial planning journey I had a lot of documents that needed signing. The adviser, probably as standard practice, sent all the documents to me, but it would have been so much easier if they had co-ordinated the signing of the documents by sending them directly to the interested parties. I didn't have the time or expertise to know what needed signing by whom. It makes much more sense (and is quicker) for the adviser to liaise directly with those who need to sign the paperwork.

52 If you're dealing with a busy business owner, always think about liaising with their secretary, personal assistant or executive assistant rather than trying to reach them directly. If you can utilise your clients' professional resources in the area of administration, it will save time for your clients, particularly when trying to get appointments in the diary.

53 If documents need returning after being signed, why not send a courier to collect them? This will save the client time and effort and greatly enhance the client experience.

54 Think about setting up an online file system for your clients, if your back office or CRM system doesn't automatically give you or them this functionality.

55 Think about giving your clients weekly updates (we call them 'client happy calls') throughout their business journey with you. On a Friday, send a text, a quick message or a voice note just to keep them updated.

56 There should never be a reason for a client to call the office. You should always remain one step ahead!

57 Do your homework on your clients and guests. It has never been easier to find out information, whether it be on Facebook, Twitter, Instagram or LinkedIn; they may even have a YouTube channel. Consider finding out who they really are, their interests, their likes, their dislikes. This will give you an opportunity to explore areas that you may not have ever thought about discussing with them, thus building great rapport and a solid foundation for a genuine long-term relationship.

58 Always remember your guest's name, the names of their family members and friends as well as any key events happening in their life. It's really important to remember the little things that are important to those who are important to us.

59 Why not have collated and designed a 'family tree' for your clients! This could be a time-consuming exercise but probably one that they wouldn't have thought of doing themselves! Big WOW!

60 Celebrate your clients' key anniversaries and dates: not just birthdays, but key dates in their journey with you. For example, you could celebrate the anniversary of their first financial planning meeting. It's an important milestone and the likelihood is that it was a meeting that actually changed their life!

61 If in the financial planning process you and the client have planned for certain key milestones, such as buying the car of their dreams, going on a round-the-world tour or even a cruise, why not get the appropriate brochures for these things to keep the client on track? Send them to remind the client that these things are still key milestones to achieve. Inspire them to stay focused!

62 Consider extending the gifts idea to clients' children or grandchildren. Children love gifts at Christmas, probably a little more than your clients do.

63 If your clients or guests often travel by taxi or car, why not set up a company taxi account so that they don't have to pay for their journey themselves? Certainly, when I've gone to pay and the driver has said, "Don't worry, it's been put on the account", it's a total WOW! moment. It shows that my hosts have cared enough about me to get me to my destination safely and not at my own cost.

64 If your clients or guests are travelling by car, arrange to valet their car while they're in a meeting with you. Don't forget to include a new air freshener and a fresh bottle of water!

65 Remember passport and driving licence expiry dates, and have application forms for both available in your office. Clients often forget ad-hoc renewal dates such as these.

66 Make sure that you remain accountable if something's gone wrong. Own up before the client finds out for themselves. Maybe an application has been sent to the wrong place, or they've been sent the wrong paperwork – don't make elaborate excuses, just apologise and rectify the situation as soon as you can. A gift or simply a card to say sorry!

67 Think about your email auto-responders and make sure that they're not just the standard reply: "I am on holiday, please contact X." Maybe look to expand that auto-responder to say that your email is very important to us, that you're sorry that you're not in the office at this moment but you're spending time with your family as it's approaching the holidays. Think about making it quirky, unique and in your company style.

68 Think about the quality of the paper that you use, both for internal and for external communications. Have printed logos on your envelopes and make sure that all the company literature is consistent. People gain huge confidence when they see that consistency is at the heart of what you do.

69 Rather than just using a franking machine, consider customising the franking stamp. You can even have personalised stamps made using the company logo or the company brand.

70 Why not host a private dinner party for your clients and their families? You can often reserve private dining areas in the nicest of restaurants. It's always good to get to know their extended family and friends!

Boosting Client Engagement

71 Communicate through social media. Comment, 'like' and share clients' posts. Advocate for their business, make introductions. Initiate conversations, share information and provide industry insight.

72 Create and publish your own blog or newsletter – provide updates on the industry and insights into your business.

73 Never underestimate the power of a handwritten note: show your gratitude and appreciation for a recent meeting or referral, or write just because you were thinking of them.

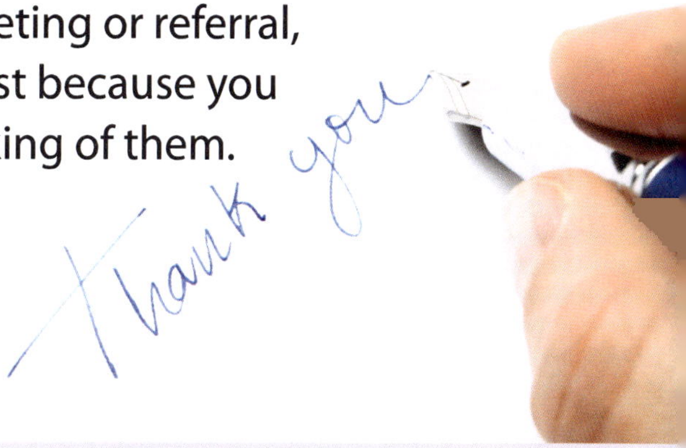

74 Everyone enjoys being surprised with a gift to celebrate their birthday, retirement, wedding or graduation. There are a variety of unique gifts that can help you score big with clients. The more bespoke and personalised you can make them, the better!

75 Send a book about personal finances to help your client better understand the financial planning process.

76 Be the first to send news on industry changes or product updates in a simple email, your newsletter or a personalised video/voice note.

77 Create personalised stationery: have personalised note cards, sticky notes, letterheads, envelopes or pens created bearing your client's name. Clients can use these year-round, and will think of you each time they do!

78 Social events present implementable, innovative marketing opportunities that require more time, but leveraging them will greatly improve your client retention, attract new clients and more than likely increase your bottom line!

79 A framed autographed photo of their favourite sports star, musician or actor will certainly be a welcome surprise! Again this may take some effort on your part, but your client will appreciate it. So find out who their favourites are and try to get a signed autograph that you can have framed.

80 A historic newspaper or magazine: find one from the day your client was born and send it as an authentic reminder of their special day. This collector's item is truly a one-of-a-kind gift.

81 Create 'retirement business cards': this unique marketing tool gives the client's contact information and a brief (humorous) note about their schedule as a retiree. The cards will read "compliments of [your firm or your name]" in the lower right corner.

82 Make a charitable donation: find out if your client has a favourite worthy cause and make a donation. Then send them a card letting them know a donation was made in their name.

83 Annual custom calendars: create a laminated one-year-view calendar with a thought-provoking financial concept, personalised with your company name and logo.

84 Office 'open house': invite clients and prospects to your office for lunch or after hours. Order food and even invite a local politician, sports figure or musician as a main speaker.

85 Why not meet with clients for lunch or dinner at one of their favourite restaurants or a new hotspot? Call ahead to arrange special treatment or the best table!

86 Surprise a client by delivering lunch for everyone in their office. Delivering it yourself is a great opportunity to meet their team and colleagues!

87 Invite your client to join you for an upcoming event, or give them a pair of tickets to a sporting event, concert, comedy show, play or ballet. If gifting a pair of tickets, offer additional tickets to be sent by you to the guest(s) of their choice.

88 Send a personalised Christmas email. Suggest they check out websites such as portablenorthpole.com, christmasdialer.com, and santatracker.google.com

89 Send a lovely holiday food recipe inside their Christmas card or within their Christmas email.

Now why not add some of your own ideas...? Never stop doing your best, never stop trying to WOW!

90 ....

91 ....

92 ....

93 ....

94 ....

95 ....

96 ....

97 ....

98 ....

99 ....

100 ....

Contact Michelle

If you would like any further information, need support in creating your perfect practice or would like to purchase any item from our best practice toolkits, please contact Michelle directly or a member of the team.

Address: 5 The Granary, Fairclough Hall Farm, Weston, Hertfordshire SG4 7DP, UK

Telephone: +44 (0)1462 790894

Website: www.standardsinternational.co.uk

Email: michelle@standardsinternational.co.uk

LinkedIn: in/standardsexpert

Twitter: @littlemisswoww

Facebook: Little Miss Woww

Instagram: Littlemisswoww

YouTube: TheStandardsExpert

MICHELLE HOSKIN is well known for her endless enthusiasm and energy, infectious personality and unique outlook on what she describes as a "magical industry". Michelle has over 15 years' experience working with some of the leading financial services practices, and is internationally recognised as the font of knowledge and the leading expert in identifying best practice standards of operation.

She designs innovative solutions proven to eliminate the debilitating challenges faced by financial services professionals every day. As a regular speaker at seminars and workshops, she stimulates and inspires her audiences with the ideas and insights that she shares with them.

Her free time is super special to her and is spent 'making home' and enjoying quality fun time with her daughter Ruby Mae!

"Michelle is an infectious bundle of energy – thank you for showering me in gold dust."

Damien Rylett, Brunel Capital Partners

"Thanks Michelle! You're fantastic! I truly appreciate your sharing of your powerful practice management tools."

Ken Royster, Metropolitan Life Insurance Company

"Thank you Michelle, I've already begun implementing some of the things you shared. Your presentation was a blessing!"

Tim Broyles, State Farm Insurance

Founded by Michelle, **Standards International is the powerhouse behind global professionalism and operational excellence in financial services.**

We support the development of financial adviser business owners, their business partners, practice and business managers, and support teams in all areas of personal and business development. Our straight-talking approach promises to push the boundaries of their potential, both personally and professionally.

Driven by our purpose we believe we each have the power to realise our extraordinary potential.

This is why we dedicate ourselves to challenging, invigorating and inspiring all those around us, so, together, we can change the world one financial adviser at a time!

"Her presentation style captivated the audience, and her delivery was inspiring. Thanks Michelle, you were awesome!"

John Lutrin, EVP, HUB Financial

"I very much appreciated you taking the time to share your best practices. I personally benefited from your unique approach to help develop a perfect practice."

Kelly Herring, Modern Woodmen of America

"(Michelle) You are the real deal!"

Tony Byrne, Wealth & Tax Management

Contact Mike

If you would like any further information about our products and ideas or for booking inquiries, please contact Mike at:

Address:	200-905 Tungsten Street Thunder Bay, ON Canada P7B 5Z3
Telephone:	1 807 684 1805
Website:	www.ideasforadvisors.com
Email:	mike@ideasforadvisors.com michelle@ideasforadvisors.com (booking inquiries)
LinkedIn:	linkedin.com/in/michaelkmorrow
Twitter:	twitter.com/_MikeMorrow_
Facebook:	facebook.com/IdeasforAdvisors
YouTube:	youtube.com/user/IdeasForAdvisors

IdeasForAdvisors.com

INNOVATIVE IDEAS TO GROW YOUR BUSINESS NOW

A widely recognized expert in sales and client appreciation, Mike shares his strategies around the globe, and many of the world's most successful professionals are using Mike's compelling ideas that get results.

As a local comic idol winner, Mike's faced-paced presentations are packed with unique ideas that are easy to remember, easy to implement and proven to give Financial Advisors income-generating results.

Mike is an International Speaker who has presented to companies all over Canada, United States, Mexico, Poland, United Kingdom, Asia, Australia and New Zealand and at Million Dollar Round Table events including MDRT UK 2015, 2012 MDRT Experience and the 2012 and 2009 MDRT Annual Meeting.

Book Mike for your next event: michelle@ideasforadvisors.com

"Mike Morrow's ideas are practical and proven to work. In his presentation, he shares strategies that truly make professionals more effective. You can't help but be more successful by picking up on his ideas."

— Tony Gordon, MDRT Past President and Top of the Table Member

"Sometimes the simpler a concept is, the more impact it will have. Mike has the ability to take complex situations and present them so simply that everybody gets it, and that includes the advisor, the client, or the professional contact you are trying to develop. Mike Morrow really is the advisors' Advisor."

— Doug Bennett, DipPFS MDRT member of 8 years with one COT qualification

Keynotes and Workshops May Include:

- Fostering client loyalty
- Generating quality inbound referrals
- Prospecting by building relationships
- Discovering meeting tools for better client understanding
- One-of-a-kind wow! strategies to make a powerful impact

CFP

Member MDRT®